PMDD
DIET GUIDE

Taking Control of Your Premenstrual Dysphoric Disorder through diet

Victoria O. Brown

TABLE OF CONTENT

INTRODUCTION

Premenstrual dysphoric disorder (PMDD) is a severe and often disabling form of premenstrual syndrome affecting up to 8% of women of reproductive age worldwide. Symptoms include depression, irritability, mood swings, insomnia, excessive fatigue, bloating, breast tenderness, and joint pain.

While there is no "cure" for PMDD, following an appropriate diet may be one way to help manage your symptoms. This PMDD Diet Guide aims to provide an understanding of PMDD and how to take control of your condition through dietary changes. Through an overview of the condition and exploring the possible dietary connections, this guide can help you determine which changes may work best for you. By taking control of your diet, you may find relief from the symptoms associated with PMDD. With this guide, you can learn how to identify the foods that may be contributing to your symptoms and what dietary changes you can make to improve your overall health and well-being.

This guide is designed to provide a comprehensive overview of PMDD and its links to diet. It will explore the potential dietary triggers for PMDD, suggest food and lifestyle modifications as possible treatments, and provide tips for managing symptoms long-term. By taking control of your diet, you can find relief from the troubling symptoms of PMDD.

For those interested in exploring the potential of a PMDD diet to reduce and manage their symptoms, this guide provides a comprehensive overview of the condition, the dietary triggers, and suggestions for making changes. With this knowledge, you can take control of your PMDD and work towards finding relief.

My neighbor was a single mother of two children. Although she wasn't wealthy, she always found ways to provide for her family and make sure they had everything they needed. She was a wonderful cook and would often invite us over for dinner to share her delicious creations.

One day, we noticed she had been looking more tired than usual and seemed a bit down in the dumps. After prodding a little, we learned that she had been diagnosed with Premenstrual Dysphoric Disorder (PMDD). She was frustrated that she couldn't seem to shake it. We suggested that she use diet as a way to take control of her PMDD and try to reduce its severity. She quickly got to work, researching, and experimenting with different dietary changes. After a few months of tweaking her diet, she finally noticed a difference in her symptoms. She was so relieved to be able to manage her PMDD without having to rely on medication.

She was an inspiration to us all. Even with her medical condition, she managed to overcome it through hard work and determination. Her story taught us that we can all take control of our health with the right lifestyle choices.

From that point on, she was a vocal advocate of using dietary changes to manage PMDD and other medical conditions. She shared her story with as many people as she could, and gave them the tools they needed to make the right dietary changes to take control of their health.

CHAPTER ONE

CAUSES OF PMDD

PMDD, also known as Premenstrual Dysphoric Disorder, is a severe form of premenstrual syndrome (PMS) that causes a range of physical, psychological, and behavioral symptoms. While the exact causes of PMDD are unknown, it is believed to be caused by a combination of hormonal and environmental factors. Hormonal imbalances are thought to play a role in the development of PMDD, as certain hormones, such as estrogen and progesterone, have been linked to the condition. Certain lifestyle factors, such as stress, lack of exercise, and poor diet, can also contribute to the development of PMDD. Additionally, there may also be a genetic component involved in the development of PMDD, as women with a family history of the condition may be more likely to develop PMDD.

It is important to note that PMDD is not a personal weakness, but rather a medical condition that requires compassionate and knowledgeable care. With the right treatment and support, women suffering from PMDD can take control of their lives and overcome this difficult condition.

Women need to take an active role in the management of their PMDD by understanding the possible causes and symptoms and seeking out appropriate treatment. By doing so, they can find the right balance in their life to manage the symptoms of PMDD and live healthy and fulfilling life.

It is important to remember that you are not alone in your battle against PMDD. There is a wealth of resources available for women seeking information about the condition and support from healthcare professionals and those who have personally experienced the impact of PMDD.

Overall, PMDD is a complex and multifaceted condition that can have both physical and psychological implications. With an understanding of the possible causes and a willingness to seek help, women dealing with PMDD can take control of their lives and manage their symptoms.

DIAGNOSING PMDD

Diagnosing Premenstrual Dysphoric Disorder (PMDD) is an important part of providing comprehensive care to women. PMDD is a debilitating condition that can cause severe physical and emotional symptoms around the time of a woman's period.

Diagnosing PMDD involves ruling out other mental health issues, taking a detailed clinical history, and understanding the importance of working collaboratively with the patient to develop an appropriate treatment plan.

The first step in diagnosing PMDD is to rule out other conditions that may be causing similar symptoms. This may involve psychological testing and evaluation, lab tests, and physical exams. Additionally, a careful review of the patient's medical records is important to look for any underlying conditions that may be contributing to the symptoms. It is also important to consider the patient's lifestyle, including their diet, level of stress, and exercise habits, as these factors can have an impact on PMDD symptoms.

Once any other causes have been ruled out, the next step in diagnosing PMDD is to take a detailed clinical history. This includes understanding the symptoms the patient is experiencing, including when they began, and how severe they are. It is also important to note relationships in the patient's life and if they have had prior episodes of depression or anxiety that may be related. Additionally, it is important to understand the patient's menstrual cycle, any medications they may be taking, and their family history.

Finally, it is important to develop an appropriate treatment plan with the patient. This may include lifestyle management strategies, such as sleep hygiene and dietary changes, as well as medications such as oral contraceptives and selective serotonin reuptake inhibitors (SSRIs). Additionally, therapy can be beneficial for some women with PMDD in helping them develop coping skills and understand their symptoms. Diagnosing PMDD requires a thorough evaluation and collaboration between the patient and the healthcare provider to ensure the best outcomes.

COMMON SYMPTOMS OF PMDD

Common symptoms of PMDD include mood swings, irritability, depression, anxiety, sleep disturbances, lethargy, breast tenderness, bloating, and food cravings. These symptoms can interfere with normal daily functioning and cause significant distress.

PMDD is believed to be caused by a combination of biological, psychological, and environmental factors. Hormones such as estrogen and progesterone can affect brain chemicals that control mood, resulting in PMDD symptoms. Stressful life events and difficult relationships can also make symptoms worse.

TREATMENT OF PMDD

There are several treatment options for PMDD. These include non-hormonal treatments such as cognitive behavioral therapy, lifestyle changes, physical activity, and relaxation techniques. Some women may benefit from antidepressant medications, such as SSRIs, SNRIs, or tricyclic antidepressants. Hormonal treatments such as oral contraceptives, progesterone-only pills, and gonadotropin-releasing hormone agonists may also be effective. It is important to speak with a healthcare provider to find the best treatment option for you.

With appropriate treatment, most women with PMDD can reduce their symptoms and lead fulfilling lives. It is important to remember that PMDD is a real medical condition and treatment should be taken seriously. If you think you may be suffering from PMDD, talk to your healthcare provider.

It is also important to remember that awareness and education are key to better-managing symptoms of PMDD. By having an open dialogue about PMDD, we can help reduce stigma and increase understanding of this condition.

CHAPTER TWO

FOOD AND PMDD

PMDD and food are two important elements that can influence one's physical and mental health. PMDD, or Premenstrual Dysphoric Disorder, is a severe form of PMS that occurs once a month in some women.

Diet and nutrition can play an important role in managing PMDD-related symptoms. Eating foods that are rich in essential nutrients and low in sugar, artificial additives, and saturated fats can help support hormone balance, reduce inflammation, and provide energy to the body. Women should opt for fresh vegetables, whole grains, lean proteins and healthy fats such as nuts and seeds. Additionally, try to reduce the amount of processed, convenience foods and alcohol.

It's also important to pay attention to portion sizes and limit snacking to avoid spikes in blood sugar levels that can worsen PMDD symptoms. Try to focus on balanced meals that include complex carbohydrates, lean proteins, and healthy fats.

In addition to dietary changes, women experiencing PMDD may benefit from incorporating natural supplements or herbs into their regimens. Magnesium, vitamin B6, omega-3 fatty acids, and chamomile are all known to help reduce PMDD-related symptoms. Speak to your doctor or healthcare provider before making any major changes to your diet or supplement regimen.

TIPS FOR EATING HEALTHILY

Making dietary changes can be difficult, but the potential benefits are worth it. Speak with a dietitian if you need help making healthy dietary choices that can benefit your overall health. With the right nutrition and lifestyle modifications, you can get your PMDD symptoms under control.

Eating healthily is an important part of managing premenstrual dysphoric disorder (PMDD). Here are a few tips to help you make healthy choices that may work best for you:

1. Eat a variety of foods. A balanced diet is essential for good health, and it's especially important for managing PMDD symptoms. Try to eat a variety of fruits, vegetables, whole grains, healthy fats, and protein sources. Eating plenty of nutrient-rich foods helps provide your body with important vitamins and minerals.

2. Watch portion sizes. While it's important to include a variety of foods in your diet, it's also important to keep portions in check. Eating too much can lead to weight gain--which can worsen PMDD symptoms. Try to measure out your portions and be aware of your calorie intake.

3. Drink plenty of water. Hydration is essential for good health, especially when you're managing PMDD. Water helps flush out toxins and helps keep you feeling healthy and energized. Try to drink at least 8 glasses of water each day.

4. Limit processed foods. Highly processed foods tend to be filled with unhealthy fats, preservatives, and other additives. These can all cause inflammation and contribute to PMDD symptoms. Aim to consume less processed foods overall and more complete, unprocessed foods

5. Eat mindfully. Eating mindfully is an important part of healthy eating. Take

time to enjoy your food and savor the flavors. Pay attention to how you're feeling when you're eating and check in with yourself to make sure you're not overeating.

By following the above tips, you can help manage your PMDD symptoms by eating a healthy and balanced diet. Remember, everybody is different and there is no one-size-fits-all approach to eating healthily. Find what works best for you and prioritize a well-rounded diet full of nutrient-rich foods.

DIET PLANS FOR MANAGING PMDD

Eat a balanced diet: Eating a variety of whole foods such as fruits, vegetables, lean proteins, and whole grains is the best way to ensure proper nutrition in managing PMDD. Eating a variety of foods provides the body with essential vitamins, minerals, and other nutrients needed to support hormonal balance and overall

Low-Fiber Diet: Premenstrual dysphoric disorder (PMDD) is a severe form of a premenstrual syndrome characterized by intense physical and emotional symptoms. These symptoms can be extremely disruptive to daily life, causing significant distress and impairing functioning. Making dietary modifications, such as following a low-fiber diet, can help manage symptoms of PMDD.

A low-fiber diet reduces the amount of dietary fiber, which is made up of carbohydrates that the body cannot digest. Dietary fiber helps to keep the digestive system regular and promotes healthy bowel movements. When someone follows a low-fiber diet, they typically limit their intake of plant-based foods, such as fresh fruit and vegetables, grains, nuts, and seeds.

The role of diet in PMDD is still not fully understood, but some research suggests that there may be a link between dietary fiber and PMDD symptoms. A low-fiber diet may help reduce bloating, cramping, and other physical symptoms associated with PMDD by reducing the amount of gas and stool that can build up in the intestines. In addition, following a low-fiber diet may help improve sleep and reduce fatigue, two common PMDD symptoms.

It's important to note that following a low-fiber diet should not be done without consulting a doctor or nutritionist. While a low-fiber diet may help manage PMDD symptoms, it's not a long-term solution and could lead to inadequate nutrient intake. A doctor or nutritionist can help create a low-fiber diet that is tailored to an individual's needs and helps ensure adequate nutrient intake.

In conclusion, making dietary modifications may help manage symptoms of PMDD. Following a low-fiber diet may reduce bloating, cramping, fatigue, and other physical and emotional symptoms associated with PMDD. However, it's important to speak with a doctor or nutritionist before starting any new diet, including a low-fiber diet.

It's also important to note that dietary modifications alone may not be enough to manage PMDD symptoms and other treatments, such as medication and psychotherapy, should also be considered.

CHAPTER THREE

MEDITERRANEAN DIET

The Mediterranean diet is a well-known healthy eating plan with proven benefits for both physical and mental health. Recent research has found that following a Mediterranean-style diet may be an effective way to manage premenstrual dysphoric disorder (PMDD).

Traditional treatments may include medications and psychotherapy, but dietary changes could provide an additional or alternative approach to help manage PMDD symptoms.

While there aren't many studies on the specific effects of a Mediterranean diet on PMDD, the diet itself can have numerous positive health effects. The diet is based on fruits, vegetables, whole grains, healthy fats, legumes, and lean proteins. It emphasizes plant-based meals and limits the intake of processed foods, red meat, and refined carbohydrates.

Research suggests that the Mediterranean diet can reduce inflammation and oxidative stress, which are thought to be associated with PMDD symptoms. Furthermore, it may help to improve cognitive functioning, which could be beneficial for women experiencing depression and anxiety associated with PMDD.

In addition to the primary components of a Mediterranean diet, some evidence suggests that adding omega-3 fatty acids (found in fish and seafood) and probiotics (found in fermented foods like yogurt or kimchi) could be beneficial for managing PMDD symptoms. Omega-3 fatty acids can help reduce inflammation and reduce the severity of PMDD symptoms, while probiotics may regulate hormones and decrease PMDD symptoms.

Ultimately, following a Mediterranean diet as part of an overall healthy lifestyle could be an effective way to manage premenstrual dysphoric disorder. While making dietary changes isn't a substitute for traditional treatments, it could be an important tool to help reduce the severity of PMDD symptoms.

Low-Sugar Diet: Low-sugar diets have been used effectively to help manage premenstrual dysphoric disorder (PMDD). PMDD is a type of PMS that can cause severe psychological symptoms such as depression and anxiety. Studies have shown that women with PMDD may benefit from dietary interventions, specifically reducing their sugar intake.

The purpose of a low-sugar diet for managing PMDD is twofold. It first aids in lowering bodily inflammation. Excess sugar consumption can cause an inflammatory response in the body which can worsen the symptoms of PMDD. Second, it helps regulate hormone levels. A diet high in sugary foods can disrupt the balance of hormones in the body, which can lead to further PMDD symptoms.

By reducing sugar intake, a low-sugar diet can help manage premenstrual dysphoric disorder (PMDD). This type of PMS can cause severe psychological symptoms such as depression and anxiety. A low-sugar diet works in two ways: it reduces inflammation in the body, which can worsen PMDD symptoms, and it helps regulate hormones, which can also cause symptoms.

There are several ways to incorporate a low-sugar diet into one's lifestyle. Start by avoiding processed and sugary foods, such as candy, cookies, cakes, sodas, and juices.

Instead, choose fresh fruits, vegetables, nuts, legumes, and whole grains. If a sweet craving hits, opt for healthy alternatives, other strategies can be incorporated into a low-sugar diet. Incorporating omega-3 fatty acids, such as those found in salmon and other cold-water fish, and healthy fats, like monounsaturated and polyunsaturated fats, can help balance hormones. Eating regular meals and snacks throughout the day can also help regulate blood sugar levels and reduce cravings. Finally, getting regular exercise helps reduce stress and promotes better overall health.

It's important to note that a low-sugar diet is not a "cure" for PMDD. It can help reduce symptoms, but only in conjunction with regular medical care and treatments, such as medications and therapy. Additionally, reducing sugar intake can have other benefits beyond PMDD management, such as improved cholesterol levels and weight loss.

For those suffering from PMDD, a low-sugar diet can make a difference. By avoiding processed and sugary foods, getting enough omega-3 fatty acids and healthy fats, eating regular meals and snacks, and exercising regularly, one may be able to reduce PMDD symptoms and live a healthier lifestyle.

NUTRITIONAL SUPPLEMENTS TO CONSIDER

Premenstrual dysphoric disorder (PMDD) is a severe form of premenstrual syndrome that affects millions of women. While the exact cause of PMDD is unknown, some nutritional supplements may help manage its symptoms. These supplements can provide extra nutrients to help balance hormones and reduce the severity of PMDD symptoms.

- Vitamin B6: Vitamin B6 is an important vitamin that helps regulate hormones. Studies have shown that supplementing with vitamin B6 may help reduce PMDD symptoms such as fatigue, irritability, mood swings, and depression. Vitamin B6 is also used to create neurotransmitters, which can further help reduce PMDD-related mood disturbances.

- Calcium: Numerous studies suggest that adding calcium to the diet can help reduce PMDD symptoms such as mood swings, depression, irritability, and anxiety. Calcium supplementation has also been shown to help reduce breast tenderness and abdominal bloating associated with PMDD. Calcium is an essential mineral that helps with the proper functioning of muscles and nerves.

- Magnesium: Magnesium is a mineral that plays a role in hormone balance as well as mood regulation. Supplementing with magnesium can help reduce symptoms of PMDD such as anxiety, irritability, depression, and fatigue. It can also reduce the duration of menstrual cramps.

- Omega-3 fatty acids: Omega-3 fatty acids are important for overall health, but they may also help reduce symptoms of PMDD such as depression, irritability, fatigue, and cognitive symptoms. Studies suggest that omega-3 fatty acids have anti-inflammatory properties, which can help reduce PMDD symptoms.

These nutritional supplements are just a few of the many options available for managing PMDD symptoms. Be sure to speak with your healthcare provider before supplementing, as some nutrients may interfere with other medications or aggravate underlying health conditions.

Other supplements that may help manage PMDD symptoms include vitamin D, zinc, folate, chaste berry, evening primrose oil, and ashwagandha. Talk to your healthcare provider about which supplements may be most beneficial for you.

CHAPTER FOUR

SAMPLE MEAL PLANS

Breakfast

A balanced diet is essential for good health, particularly for those with the premenstrual dysphoric disorder (PMDD). Eating a healthy and varied meal plan can help manage symptoms of PMDD. Here are 20 sample breakfast ideas to help with PMDD management:

1. Oats with banana, honey, and cinnamon.
2. Greek yogurt with fresh berries, nuts, and seeds.
3. Avocado toast with tomatoes and feta.

4. Egg muffin cups with vegetables and shredded cheese.
5. Whole-grain pancakes with nut butter.
6. Tofu scramble with mushrooms, bell peppers, and onions.
7. Smoothie bowl with chia seeds
8. Egg and vegetable breakfast burrito.
9. Açai bowl with fresh berries, almonds, and coconut flakes.
10. Protein oatmeal muffins with apples and walnuts.
11. Whole-grain waffles with peanut butter and banana.
12. Baked oatmeal with blueberries and walnuts.
13. Quinoa egg bake with spinach and tomatoes.
14. Chia pudding with almond milk and diced apples.

15. Steel-cut oats with dates, figs, and walnuts.

16. Savory oatmeal with broccoli, sunflower seeds, and cheese.

17. Breakfast parfait with yogurt, granola, and fruit.

18. Avocado toast with tomatoes and feta.

19. Sweet potato muffins with dates and pecans.

20. Coconut chia pudding with pomegranate and almonds.

Try different combinations of ingredients to create your nourishing morning meals.

Lunch

Here are 20 sample meal plans for managing PMDD:

1. A breakfast bowl with oatmeal, nuts, seeds, and dried fruit.
2. Blueberry smoothie with spinach, Greek yogurt, almond milk, and flaxseeds.
3. Whole grain toast with peanut butter and banana slices.
4. Egg and vegetable omelet with feta cheese.
5. Avocado toast on whole grain bread.
6. A hearty salad with quinoa, roasted veggies, and feta cheese.
7. Salmon and brown rice bowl with steamed vegetables.
8. Baked sweet potato with black beans, spinach, and avocado.
9. Chickpea curry with brown basmati rice and roasted vegetables.

10. Tuna salad wrapped with Greek yogurt dressing.

11. Sushi bowl with avocado and edamame.

12. Lentil soup with quinoa and roasted vegetables.

13. Hummus and veggie wrap in a whole wheat tortilla.

14. Zucchini noodles with grilled chicken and pesto sauce.

15. Veggie burgers with sweet potato fries.

16. Greek yogurt parfait with granola, banana slices, and chia seed.

17. Oven-baked fish with boiled potatoes and steamed broccoli.

18. Quinoa and black bean burrito bowl with tomatoes, lettuce, and avocado.

19. Spaghetti squash with grilled chicken and tomato sauce.

20. Air-fried falafels with cucumber, tomato, and tzatziki sauce.

Eating healthy and balanced meals can also help boost your energy levels, regulate your moods, and manage stress. Planning is essential for maintaining a healthy diet, so make sure to create or follow sample meal plans to ensure that your nutritional needs are met and you're managing PMDD symptoms effectively.

Dinner

Following a meal plan can be an effective way to manage the symptoms of Premenstrual Dysphoric Disorder (PMDD).

To help you get started, here are 20 dinner ideas that are designed to provide your body with the nutrients it needs to function properly.

1. **Grilled Salmon with Roasted Asparagus and Wild Rice**: Salmon is a great source of Omega-3 fatty acids, which have been linked to improved mood and reduced symptoms of PMDD. Asparagus is high in folate, an important B vitamin, and wild rice is a complex carbohydrate that will provide sustained energy.

PREPARATION METHOD:

- Start by preheating the oven to 400 degrees Fahrenheit.

- Place the wild rice in a pot and cover it with two inches of water.
- Bring to a boil and reduce to a simmer, then cover and cook for 35 minutes.
- When the rice is cooked, remove it from the heat and add the asparagus.
- Drizzle with olive oil, sprinkle with salt and pepper,
- Then bake for 20 minutes.
- Heat a lightly oiled grill over medium-high heat and season the salmon with salt and pepper.
- Grill each side for 5 to 6 minutes, or until well done.
- Serve the grilled salmon over a bed of wild rice and roasted asparagus and enjoy

2. **Quinoa Stuffed Peppers with Spinach and Chickpeas**: This tasty vegan dinner is packed with a variety of vitamins and minerals. Quinoa is a great source of complete protein, spinach is high in folate, and chickpeas provide iron and magnesium.

PREPARATION METHOD

- Preheat oven to 375 degrees Fahrenheit and prepare a baking sheet with parchment paper.

- In a medium saucepan, cook 1 cup of quinoa according to the package instructions.

- Meanwhile, in a large skillet, heat 2 tablespoons of olive oil over medium-high heat.

- Add 1 chopped onion to the skillet and sauté until softened, about 5 minutes.

- Add 1 teaspoon of ground cumin, 1 teaspoon of smoked paprika, a pinch of cayenne pepper, 1/2 teaspoon of salt, 1/4 teaspoon of black pepper, and 2 cloves of minced garlic to the skillet. Cook for 1 minute, stirring frequently.

- Add 1/2 cup of cooked chickpeas, 2 cups of packed spinach, 1/4 cup of raisins, and 1/4 cup of sliced almonds to the skillet. Cook for three to four minutes, or until the spinach wilts.

- Reduce the heat to low and add the cooked quinoa to the skillet. Stir to combine.

- Cut 4 bell peppers in half lengthwise, remove the stems and seeds, and place them on the prepared baking sheet.

- Divide the quinoa filling among the 4 bell pepper halves.
- Bake for 20 minutes until the peppers are tender.

3. **Lentil Soup with Sweet Potatoes and Kale:** Lentils are a great plant-based source of protein and are also high in iron and magnesium. Sweet potatoes contain beta-carotene, an important antioxidant, and kale provides vitamin K and other nutrients.

PREPARATION METHOD

- Heat 2 tablespoons of olive oil to medium-high heat in a big saucepan.

- Add 1 chopped onion and 2 cloves of minced garlic to the pot and sauté until softened, about 5 minutes.

- Add 2 cups of dried green or brown lentils, 8 cups of vegetable broth, 1 large sweet potato (peeled and diced), 1 teaspoon of dried oregano, and 1 teaspoon of dried thyme to the pot. Bring to a boil, then turn down the heat to a low simmer for 20 minutes with a lid on.

- Add 1 bunch of chopped kale, 1/2 teaspoon of salt, and 1/ 4 teaspoon of black pepper to the pot. Lentils should be soft after 10 minutes of simmering with the cover on.

- Serve hot with freshly chopped parsley, if desired.

4. **Grilled Chicken Salad with Avocado and Walnuts:** The protein from the chicken will help to maintain your energy levels, and the healthy fats from the avocado and walnuts can help to improve your mood.

PREPARATION METHOD

- Set the oven's temperature to 375° F.
- Place the chicken breasts in an oven-safe dish, season with salt and pepper, and cook for 25 minutes, or until cooked through.
- Make the salad while the chicken is cooking. Arrange the lettuce, avocado, walnuts, and tomatoes on a large plate.

- When the chicken is done, let it cool for a few minutes before slicing it into strips.
- Top the salad with the chicken strips, then drizzle with your desired amount of olive oil and balsamic vinegar.
- Serve and enjoy.

5. **Almond Crusted Fish with Garlic Roasted Broccoli and Quinoa:** This dinner combines the protein from the fish and quinoa with the anti-inflammatory benefits of garlic and vitamin K from the broccoli.

PREPARATION METHOD

- Put a baking sheet in the oven and preheat the oven to 425°F.

- In a shallow bowl, mix almond meal, salt, pepper, and garlic powder until combined.
- Rinse the fish fillets and pat dry. Dip each fillet into the almond mixture and coat evenly on both sides. Place the almond-crusted fish on the prepared baking sheet.
- Bake in the preheated oven for 12-15 minutes or until cooked through.
- While the fish is cooking, prepare the roasted broccoli by tossing broccoli florets with garlic, olive oil
- Spread the broccoli on a baking sheet and roast in the oven at 425°F for 20 minutes.
- Meanwhile, bring a pot of salted water to a boil and add the quinoa. For about 15 minutes, simmer the grains

until they are soft. Drain the quinoa before transferring it to a serving bowl.

- Once the fish and broccoli are cooked, assemble the dish by adding the roasted broccoli and fish to the quinoa. Serve warm with lemon wedges. Enjoy!

6. **Turkey Burgers with Sweet Potato Fries and Spinach:** Turkey is a great source of lean protein and B vitamins, while sweet potatoes are high in beta-carotene and spinach provides folate and other vitamins.

PREPARATION METHOD

- Preheat the oven to 400°F (200°C).

- Slice the sweet potatoes into thin fries and place them on a baking sheet. Drizzle with olive oil, salt, and pepper, and bake for 20-25 minutes or until golden brown.
- Meanwhile, heat a skillet over medium-high heat. Use the ground turkey to make 4 patties, then salt and pepper them. Add to the pan and cook for about 8 minutes per side, or until cooked through.
- When the sweet potato fries are finished, turn the oven temperature to broil. Place the burgers in an oven-safe dish and top with American cheese slices. The cheese has to be melted and bubbling after about 5 minutes under the broiler.

- Heat a separate skillet over medium heat with a little oil. When the spinach has wilted, add it and simmer for another two to three minutes.

- Serve the burgers on buns (or lettuce wraps) with the sweet potato fries, spinach, and any other desired toppings. Enjoy!

7. **Grilled Tempeh with Roasted Brussels Sprouts and Brown Rice**: Tempeh is a great vegan source of complete protein, and the combination of Brussels sprouts and brown rice provides your body with essential nutrients like vitamins C and B6.

PREPARATION METHOD

- Preheat the oven to 400°F (200°C).
- Slice the tempeh into 1/2-inch thick slices and place on a baking sheet. Olive oil should be drizzled on top of the seasoning salt and pepper.
- Place the baking sheet in the oven and roast for 20 minutes.
- Meanwhile, prepare the Brussels sprouts by washing and trimming off the tough ends. Add salt and pepper, then toss in the olive oil. Place on a separate baking sheet and place in the oven with the tempeh. Roast for 20 minutes.
- Cook the brown rice according to package instructions.
- Heat a non-stick skillet over medium heat and lightly grease with olive oil. Add the tempeh slices and cook until

both sides are golden brown, about 2-3 minutes per side.

- Divide the cooked brown rice, roasted Brussels sprouts, and grilled tempeh between four plates and serve. Enjoy!

8. **Grilled Pork Tenderloin with Zucchini Noodles and Mushrooms**: This flavorful dinner provides your body with essential vitamins and minerals like folate and B vitamins from the pork and mushrooms. Zucchini noodles are a low-calorie, low-carbohydrate option that is packed with vitamins A and B6.

PREPARATION METHOD

- Preheat the grill to medium-high heat.

- Trim any excess fat from the pork tenderloin and season with salt and pepper.
- Place the pork tenderloin on the preheated grill and cook for about 8 minutes per side, or until it reaches an internal temperature of 145°F (63°C).
- Meanwhile, make the zucchini noodles using a spiralizer. Heat a drizzle of olive oil in a skillet over medium-high heat and add the zucchini noodles. Sauté for 3-4 minutes or until they are slightly softened. Transfer
- Add the mushrooms to the skillet with the zucchini noodles and sauté for an additional 3-4 minutes. Season with salt and pepper.

- When the pork is done, remove it from the grill and allow it to rest for 5 minutes before slicing.
- Plate the sliced pork tenderloin, the zucchini noodles and mushrooms, and the Brussels sprouts and serve. Enjoy!

9. **Baked Salmon with Tomatoes and Orzo:** Tomatoes provide vitamins C and A, and orzo is a great source of energy. Salmon also contains healthy omega-3 fatty acids, which can help to reduce the symptoms of PMDD.

PREPARATION METHOD

- Preheat the oven to 400°F (204°C).

- Place the salmon in a shallow baking dish and season with salt, pepper, and other desired spices or herbs.
- Arrange the tomato slices around the salmon.
- Drizzle with olive oil and sprinkle with fresh or dried herbs.
- preheated the oven and bake for 15 minutes.
- Meanwhile, heat a pot of salted water on the stove. Once boiling, add orzo and cook, stirring occasionally, until al dente, about 9-11 minutes.
- Drain the cooked orzo and return it to the pot.
- Add the cooked orzo to the baking dish with the salmon and tomatoes.

- Stir in additional seasonings, such as salt, pepper, or fresh herbs.

- Bake in preheated oven until salmon is cooked through and orzo is lightly browned about 10-15 minutes.

- Serve immediately. Enjoy!

10. **Spaghetti Squash with Turkey Meatballs and Spinach:** This meal combines the protein from the turkey with the vitamin. This meal combines the protein from the turkey with vitamin K and other nutrients from the spinach. Spaghetti squash is a low-carbohydrate, nutrient-dense alternative to traditional spaghetti.

PREPARATION METHOD

- Preheat the oven to 375°F (190°C).

- Scoop out the seeds after cutting the spaghetti squash in half lengthwise.
- Brush the inside of each squash half lightly with oil and season with salt and pepper.
- Place the halves cut side down in a baking dish and bake for 25 minutes.
- While the squash is baking, prepare the meatballs. In a large bowl, mix ground turkey, breadcrumbs, minced garlic, egg, Parmesan cheese, and any desired herbs or spices.
- Form into meatballs and place on a baking sheet lined with parchment paper.
- Bake in preheated oven for 15-20 minutes, or until cooked through.

- Heat a large skillet over medium heat and add a drizzle of oil.

- Add the spinach and cook, stirring often, until lightly wilted, about 2-3 minutes.

- When the spaghetti squash is done baking, use a fork to scrape out the strands of squash.

- Divide the spaghetti squash between two plates.

- Top each plate with half of the spinach, then add half of the meatballs.

- Serve immediately. Enjoy!

11. **Lentil Tacos with Avocado and Bell Peppers**: Lentils are high in fiber, iron, and magnesium, while avocado and bell peppers provide an

array of vitamins and minerals. You can add some hot sauce to kick up the flavor.

PREPARATION METHOD

- In a medium pot, add lentils and cover with 1 inch of water.
- Bring to a boil, reduce heat, and simmer for about 20 minutes, or until the lentils are tender.
- Drain and set aside.
- Heat a large skillet over medium heat and add a drizzle of oil.
- Add diced bell peppers and cook until softened, about 5 minutes.
- Add cooked lentils, cumin, chili powder, garlic powder, and a pinch of salt and pepper. Stir to combine.

- Cook for an additional 3-5 minutes, stirring often.
- Heat a separate skillet over medium heat
- Add oil and warm tortillas, one at a time, flipping after 1 minute.
- Slice the avocado and prepare any additional desired toppings, such as tomatoes, diced onions, fresh cilantro, or jalapeños.
- To assemble tacos, fill each tortilla with the lentil-bell pepper mixture, and top with avocado slices and other desired toppings.
- Serve immediately. Enjoy!

12. **Grilled Vegetable Skewers with Quinoa Pilaf:** This vegan dinner is full of vitamins, minerals, and healthy

plant-based protein. The quinoa pilaf adds a delicious nutty flavor.

PREPARATION METHOD

- Grill or grill pan should be heated to medium-high.
- Prepare the vegetable skewers by threading the vegetables onto the skewers. This can be done with any combination of vegetables, such as bell peppers, mushrooms, zucchini, and onion.
- Place the vegetable skewers on the preheated grill or grill pan. Cook for 3-4 minutes per side, or until lightly charred and tender.
- Meanwhile, prepare the quinoa pilaf. Heat a pot over medium heat and add a drizzle of olive oil.

- Add diced onions and cook until softened, about 5 minutes.
- Stir in the uncooked quinoa
- Add water, bring to a boil, reduce to simmer, and cook for 15 minutes, or until quinoa is tender and the liquid is absorbed.
- Once the quinoa is cooked, fluff it with a fork and stir in any desired seasonings, such as salt, pepper, or fresh herbs.
- Serve the grilled vegetable skewers atop the quinoa pilaf.
- Enjoy!

13. **Stir-Fry with Tofu and Broccoli**: This dinner is packed with protein from the tofu and vitamins from the broccoli. You can add a variety of

spices and other vegetables to make it even tastier.

PREPARATION METHOD

- Prepare the tofu by draining and pressing it to remove excess liquid.
- Cut it into cubes and season with desired spices or sauces.
- A large skillet or wok should be heated well. Add some oil and give it a quick spin to coat.
- Add cubed tofu and cook, stirring occasionally, for about 4-5 minutes, or until golden and slightly crispy.
- Tofu should be taken out of the pan and placed aside.

- Add a little more oil to the pan and add the broccoli florets.

- Stir-fry for 2-3 minutes, or until lightly browned and tender.
- Return the tofu
- Add desired sauces or seasonings, such as soy sauce or garlic-ginger paste.
- Stir-fry for an additional 2 minutes, until everything is thoroughly combined and heated through.
- Serve the stir-fry in bowls with desired accompaniments, such as steamed rice or noodles.
- Enjoy!

14. **Lentil Curry with Zucchini and Eggplant:** Lentils are a great source of protein and fiber, while zucchini and eggplant provide vitamins A and

C. You can add some coconut milk for an extra creamy texture.

PREPARATION METHOD

- Heat a large pot over medium heat and add a drizzle of oil.
- Add diced onion and cook until softened, about 5 minutes.
- Add minced garlic and cook for an additional minute.
- Stir in the curry powder, cumin, turmeric, and a pinch of salt and pepper.
- Add the diced zucchini and eggplant and stir to combine.
- Pour in the lentils and vegetable broth and bring to a simmer.

- Reduce heat and let simmer, stirring occasionally, for about 25 minutes, or until the lentils are softened and the liquid has reduced.
- Serve the lentil curry with steamed rice, warmed naan bread, or other desired accompaniments.
- Enjoy!

15. **Grilled Halibut with Sweet Potato Fries and Kale:** Halibut provides essential omega-3 fatty acids, sweet potatoes are high in beta-carotene, and kale provides vitamin K and other nutrients.

PREPARATION METHOD

- Grill or grill pan should be heated to medium-high

- Cut the sweet potatoes into french fry shapes, toss with a drizzle of oil, and season with salt and pepper.
- Place the sweet potato fries on the preheated grill or grill pan and cook for 8-10 minutes, flipping halfway through.
- Meanwhile, season the halibut fillets with desired herbs, spices, and salt and pepper.
- Add the halibut to the preheated grill or grill pan and cook for about 4-5 minutes per side, or until cooked through.
- Heat a large skillet over medium heat and add a drizzle
- Add diced onions and cook until softened, about 5 minutes.

- Stir in the kale and a pinch of salt and pepper. Cook, stirring occasionally until lightly wilted, about 2-3 minutes.
- Serve the grilled halibut with the sweet potato fries and kale.
- Enjoy!

16. **Quinoa Bowl with Baked Tofu and Roasted Vegetables**: This vegan meal is loaded with vitamins and minerals from the quinoa, tofu, and roasted vegetables. It will provide your body with sustained energy throughout the day.

PREPARATION METHOD
- Preheat the oven to 400°F (204°C).

- Cut your desired vegetables into bite-sized pieces and spread them on a baking sheet.
- Drizzle with a little oil, season with salt and pepper, and toss to combine.
- Roast in preheated oven for 15-20 minutes, or until lightly browned and tender.
- Meanwhile, prepare the tofu. Drain and press the tofu to remove excess liquid. Cut it into cubes and season with desired spices or sauces.
- Place the cubed tofu on a baking sheet and bake in preheated oven for 15-20 minutes, or until golden and crispy.
- Heat a pot over medium heat and add a drizzle of oil.

- Add diced onions and cook until softened, about 5 minutes.
- Stir in the uncooked quinoa and toast for 1 minute.
- Pour in water, bring to a boil, reduce to a simmer, and cook for 15 minutes, or until quinoa is tender and the liquid is absorbed.
- Divide the cooked quinoa between two bowls. Top with roasted vegetables, baked tofu, and any desired accompaniments, such as diced tomatoes, fresh herbs, or pickled onions.
- Enjoy!

17. **Portobello Mushroom Burgers with Spinach Salad:** Portobello mushrooms are a great source of

protein, and spinach provides folate and other vitamins. You can add other salad veggies for extra flavor and nutrition.

PREPARATION METHOD

- Preheating the oven to 400 degrees F
- Place 4 portobello mushrooms on a baking sheet and brush each with 2 tablespoons of olive oil.
- Sprinkle salt and pepper to the mushrooms.
- Roast the mushrooms in the oven for 12 minutes, flipping them halfway through.
- Meanwhile, prepare the spinach salad. In a large bowl, combine 2 cups of spinach leaves, 1/2 cup of cherry tomatoes, 1/4 cup of sliced red onion,

and 2 tablespoons of chopped fresh herbs (such as basil or parsley).

- In a small bowl, whisk together 1/4 cup of olive oil, 2 tablespoons of red wine vinegar, 1 tablespoon of honey, and 1 teaspoon of Dijon mustard.
- After adding the dressing, mix the salad to incorporate.
- When the mushrooms are done roasting, let them cool for a few minutes.
- Place each mushroom on a bun and top with the spinach salad. Serve immediately.

18. **Chili with Black Beans and Sweet Potatoes:** This comforting dinner is full of muscle-building protein from the black beans and

beta-carotene from the sweet potatoes. You can add some bell peppers or corn for extra flavor.

PREPARATION METHOD

- Begin by gathering all the necessary ingredients: 2 pounds ground beef, 1 large onion (diced), 2 cloves garlic (minced), 2 teaspoons ground cumin, 2 teaspoons dried oregano, 1 teaspoon smoked paprika, 1 teaspoon chili powder, 1 teaspoon salt, 4 cups beef broth, 2 (14.5-ounce) cans diced tomatoes, 2 (15.5-ounce) cans black beans (drained and rinsed), 2 medium sweet potatoes (peeled and cut into ½-inch cubes).

- To cook the chili, heat a large pot over medium-high heat. Add the ground beef and cook for 8-10 minutes, breaking it up with a wooden spoon
- Add the diced onion and garlic and cook for an additional 3-4 minutes, until the onions are softened.
- Add the cumin, oregano, paprika, chili powder, and salt to the pot and stir to combine.
- Add the beef broth and diced tomatoes to the pot and stir to combine. Then turn down the heat to low after bringing the mixture to a boil. Simmer for 20-30 minutes, stirring occasionally.
- Add the black beans and sweet potatoes to the pot and stir to combine. Cook the potatoes for a

further 20 minutes or until they are soft.

- Taste and adjust the seasoning if necessary. Serve the chili with your favorite Toppings, such as fresh cilantro, diced avocado, sour cream, grated cheese, and diced onions. Enjoy!

19. **Poached Salmon with Roasted Brussels Sprouts and Quinoa**: Salmon is a great source of omega-3 fatty acids, while Brussels sprouts and quinoa provide an array of vitamins and minerals. You can top it off with a squeeze of lemon for extra flavor.

PREPARATION METHOD

- Preheat the oven to 425°F (220°C).

- In a large saucepan, bring the 2 cups of water, white wine, lemon juice, garlic, dill, 1/2 teaspoon of salt, and 1/4 teaspoon of black pepper to a simmer.
- Place the salmon fillet in the simmering liquid, making sure it is fully submerged. Cover and simmer for about 8-10 minutes, or until the salmon is cooked through.
- Remove the salmon from the liquid and set it aside to cool.
- In a large mixing bowl, toss the Brussels sprouts with 2 tablespoons of olive oil, 1/4 teaspoon of salt, and 1/4 teaspoon of black pepper.
- Spread the Brussels sprouts on a baking sheet and roast them in the preheated oven for about 20-25

minutes, or until they are golden brown and tender.

- In a medium saucepan, bring the 2 cups of water and 1/4 teaspoon of salt to a boil.
- Add the rinsed and drained quinoa to the boiling water, reduce the heat to low, cover, and simmer for about 18-20 minutes, or until the water is absorbed and the quinoa is tender.
- Fluff the quinoa with a fork and divide it among plates.
- Arrange the poached salmon and roasted Brussels sprouts on top of the quinoa.
- Serve and enjoy!

Note: You can also add some herbs or spices like thyme or paprika to the quinoa or fish for more flavor.

20. **Sheet Pan Fish and Veggies:** This dinner is easy to make and full of essential nutrients. Choose your favorite fish, such as salmon or cod, and any combination of vegetables like bell peppers, squash, and zucchini.

PREPARATION METHOD

- Preheat the oven to 425°F (220°C).
- In a small mixing bowl, combine 1/4 cup of olive oil, lemon juice, oregano, 1/2 teaspoon of salt, and 1/4 teaspoon of black pepper.
- Cut the fish fillet into 4 equal portions and place them on a sheet pan.
- Apply the blended olive oil on the fish
- Cut the vegetables into bite-sized pieces and add them to the sheet pan.

- Add minced garlic, 1 tablespoon of olive oil, 1/4 teaspoon of salt, and 1/4 teaspoon of black pepper to the vegetables and toss to combine.
- Arrange the fish and vegetables in a single layer on the sheet pan.
- Roast in the preheated oven for about 15-20 minutes, or until the fish is cooked through and the vegetables are tender.
- Serve and enjoy!

Note: You can also use any type of fish or vegetable of your choice.

These meals are all nutrient-dense, delicious options that can help to manage the symptoms of PMDD. They are also quick and easy to prepare, so you can focus on taking care of yourself

CHAPTER FIVE

BENEFIT OF A PMDD DIET

If you are suffering from premenstrual dysphoric disorder (PMDD), then making some dietary changes can help reduce the severity and frequency of your symptoms. Eating a premenstrual dysphoric diet (PMDD diet) can help reduce the symptoms of PMDD and improve your overall health.

A PMDD diet is a special kind of diet that is designed to reduce the symptoms of PMDD. It focuses on foods that are high in nutrients and low in processed foods, sugar, and caffeine. It also encourages the consumption of foods that contain essential fatty acids, complex carbohydrates, and vitamins and minerals.

The main benefit of a PMDD diet is that it can help reduce the severity and frequency of your symptoms. Eating a balanced diet can provide your body with the nutrients it needs to function properly and stay healthy. Eating a diet that is rich in essential fatty acids can help reduce inflammation, which can help lessen the symptoms of PMDD. Additionally, eating complex carbohydrates can help stabilize your blood sugar levels, which can help reduce the fatigue associated with PMDD.

Another benefit of a PMDD diet is that it can help reduce stress. Eating foods that are high in fiber, vitamins, and minerals can help reduce stress levels. Additionally, eating foods that are high in protein can help you feel fuller for longer and allow your body to better cope with stress.

Finally, a PMDD diet can also help improve your overall health. Your body can get the nutrients it needs to function effectively by eating a balanced diet. Additionally, eating a diet that is low in processed foods and high in healthy foods can help reduce your risk of developing chronic health conditions, such as heart disease and diabetes.

If you are suffering from PMDD, then making some dietary changes can help reduce the severity and frequency of your symptoms. Eating a premenstrual dysphoric diet can help reduce the symptoms of PMDD and improve your overall health.

CONCLUSION

In conclusion, managing PMDD through diet is a great way to take control of your premenstrual dysphoric disorder. Eating a healthy, balanced diet, understanding the causes of PMDD, recognizing the common symptoms, and understanding the benefits of a PMDD diet plan are all key to managing PMDD effectively. By incorporating the nutritional supplements and Mediterranean diet discussed in this book into your lifestyle, you can make a positive change in your overall health and well-being. With the correct diet and lifestyle changes, you can have a healthier and happier life.